Rabbit Stew

JADE RUTTER

ISBN 979-8-89243-643-4 (paperback)
ISBN 979-8-88943-960-8 (hardcover)
ISBN 979-8-88943-961-5 (digital)

Copyright © 2024 by Jade Rutter

All rights reserved. No part of this publication may be reproduced, distributed, or transmitted in any form or by any means, including photocopying, recording, or other electronic or mechanical methods without the prior written permission of the publisher. For permission requests, solicit the publisher via the address below.

Christian Faith Publishing
832 Park Avenue
Meadville, PA 16335
www.christianfaithpublishing.com

Printed in the United States of America

"Dedicated to my son Charles and five siblings. Whether near or far you're always within my heart." Jeremiah 1:5

PRODUCE
FOR
SALE!

My name is Rabbit Stew, but you can call me Stew for short.
I moved into my newest pad on February 7th, a Tuesday.

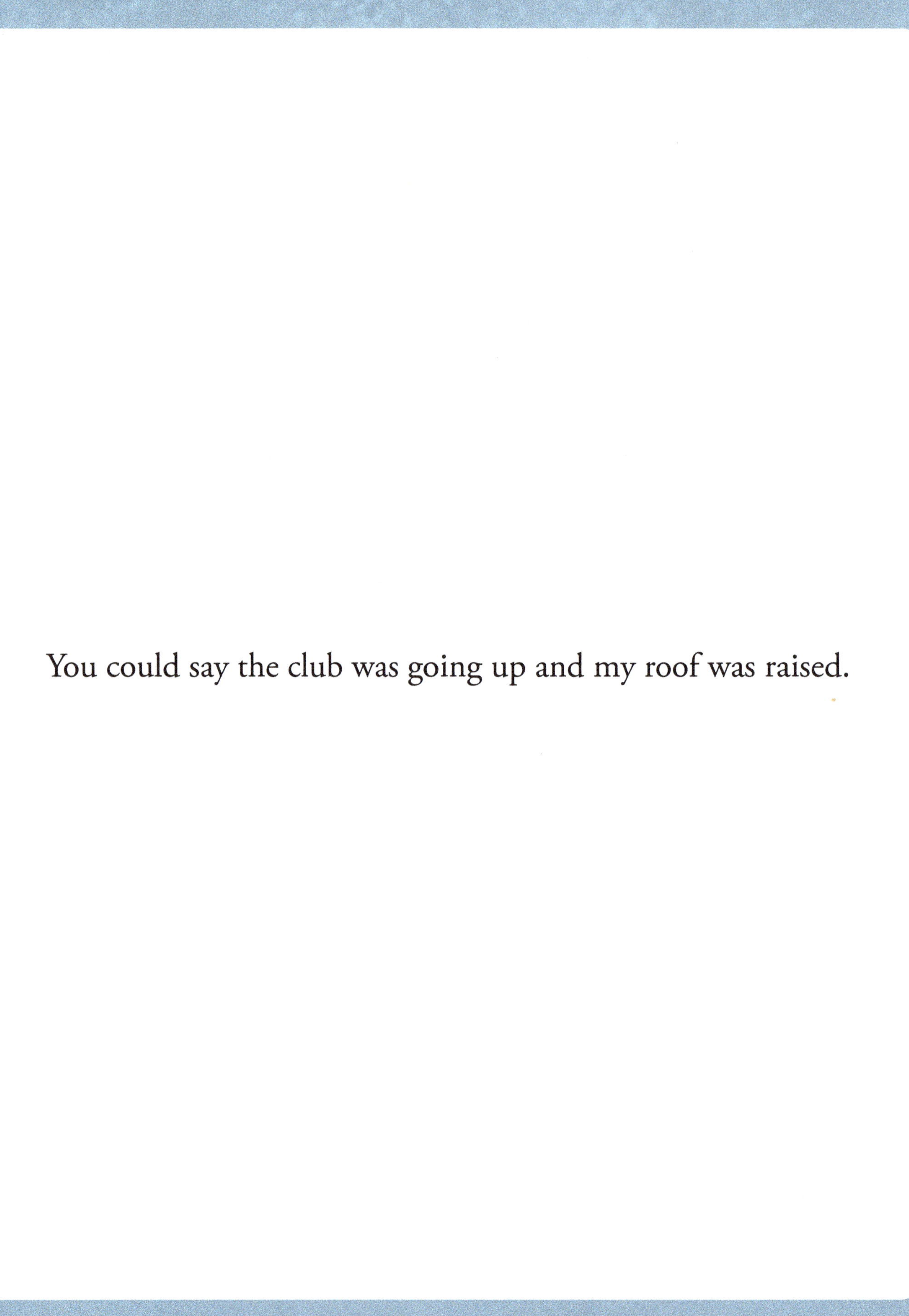
You could say the club was going up and my roof was raised.

We bought a Rabbit!
Okay

I live with two quirky adults who make fast decisions
Or rather one, and the other just goes along with it.

There is also a small boy who brings me rabbit treats and fills my bowl with hay.
Life is pretty good to me these days
But it didn't start out that way!

3RD

I was a farm project. I was shown in the fair last year, but I didn't win.
My owners were going to make me into rabbit stew!

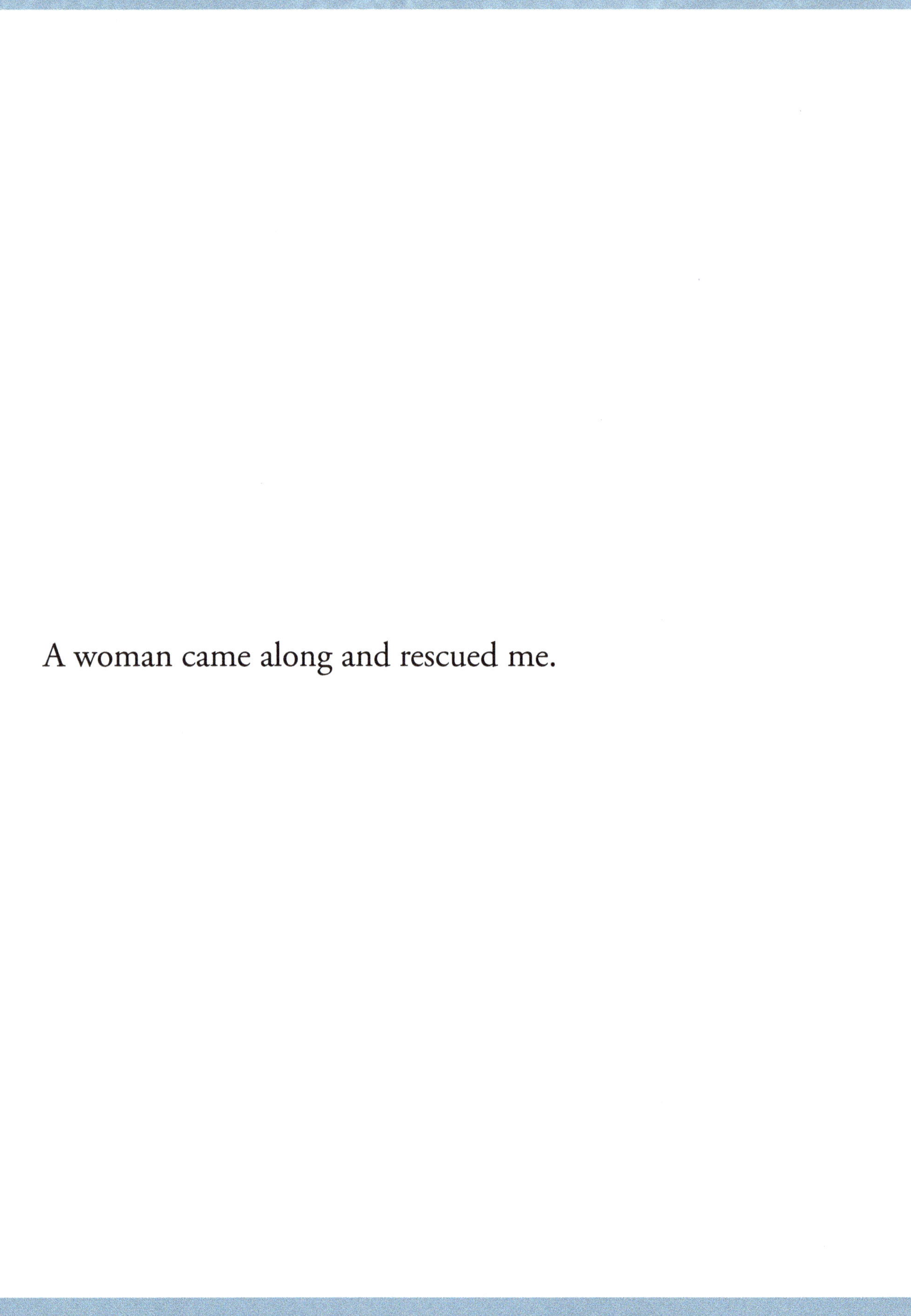

A woman came along and rescued me.

Is your Rabbit still for sale?
Yes he is!

She took me to live with someone else for a little while.
I loved the little ones who would come up and play with me
each day,

But they have a dog, and he tried to eat through my cage!

RABBIT NEEDS
FOREVER HOME!
DOG TRIES EATING RABBIT CAGE!
I CAN DIG MY OWN HOLE
THANK YOU!

They decided that they wouldn't be able to help me anymore

So they asked around and found me a new home.
Right across the street!
I get to see the little ones who I hold so dear,

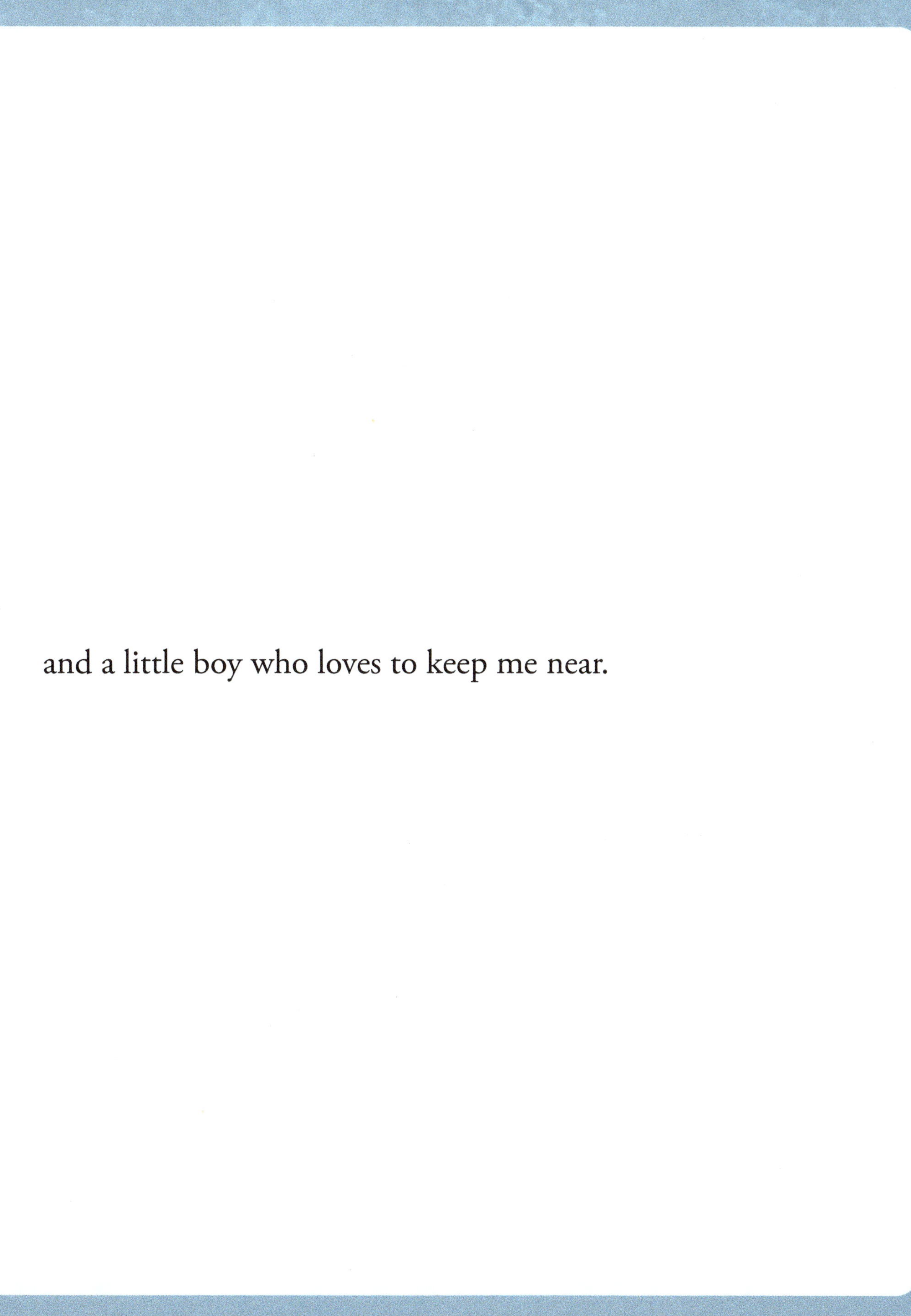

and a little boy who loves to keep me near.

So if you're like me,
and searching for a place that you can call home
Just wait and see
This life of ours works out the way it is supposed to be!

Home
SWEET
Homestead

About the Author

For the past twenty-seven years, Jade Rutter has lived in the heart of Ohio. She's an avid collector of yarn and crochet hooks and has a fondness for animals including her guinea pigs, rabbit, cats, husband, and son, Charlie. She spends her days caring for Parkinson's patients, tending to her garden and napping.

Like Rabbit Stew, she has endured many trials and tribulations throughout her life. With God and the help of kind strangers, she weathered each storm and has found her forever home. She holds out hope that each reader will too. Her favorite message to spread is that we are never alone when we have God.

www.ingramcontent.com/pod-product-compliance
Lightning Source LLC
Chambersburg PA
CBHW040200110726
48005CB00018B/2834